Growing Old
Disgracefully

Growing Old
Disgracefully

ROHAN CANDAPPA

TED SMART

This edition published in 2006 for The Book People Ltd,
Hall Wood Avenue, Haydock, St Helens, WA11 0UL

1 3 5 7 9 10 8 6 4 2

First published in 2002 by Ebury Press, an imprint of Ebury Publishing

Ebury Publishing is a division of the Random House Group

The Random House Group Limited Reg. No. 954009

Addresses for companies within the Random House Group can be found at
www.randomhouse.co.uk

A CIP catalogue record for this book is available from the British Library

The Random House Group Limited makes every effort to ensure that
the papers used in our books are made from trees that have been legally
sourced from well-managed and credibly certified forests. Our paper
procurement policy can be found on www.randomhouse.co.uk

Printed and bound in Great Britain by Mackays of Chatham Plc

ISBN 0091915252
ISBN 9780091915254 (from Jan 2007)

For Leslie & Beulah, Bob & Audrey,
George & Mano, Harry & Eileen,
Barbara & Dennis, Dolly & Michael,
Bobby & Joy, Patrick & Mary,
Susie & Graham, Denzil & Carmen,
and Sunno.

Thank you for all the things you have
shown me and for all the times you
have shared with me.

Do not go gentle into that good night,
Old age should burn and rave at close of day;
Rage, rage against the dying of the light.

DYLAN THOMAS

You're all doing very well ...

YOUNG MR GRACE

Introduction

Where's the fun in growing old gracefully? Far better to put your name down for a course of bad behaviour, irresponsibility and questionable fashion choices. And anything that winds your kids up must be worth having a crack at. On top of all that, what better way to keep the Grim Reaper from knocking at your door than having the miserable sod doubled up with laughter?

A simple piece of arithmetic

If life begins at 40, then a 60 year old is not yet 21. And think how much mayhem still lay ahead of you at that age. Act accordingly.

Seize the day

If you want to do something, do it. Don't
worry if it's right or wrong. Don't worry
whether it will work out or not. And above all
else don't worry what other people will think.
Especially if their disapproval is based upon
outdated and insulting preconceptions of what
age means. So go to those salsa lessons, dye
your hair platinum blonde, and buy that saucy
basque.

And as for you ladies ...

Seizure the day

Faking a heart attack is always a good way of
getting some attention, or livening up an
otherwise dull social occasion.

You're not going out dressed like that!

Remember all that awful stuff that your kids insisted on wearing when they were teenagers? And the grief that you went through whenever they went out looking like an explosion in a jumble sale, or an overconfident peacock who took Liberace as a role model, or a juvenile hooker who'd been kicked out of Sodom and Gomorrah for lowering the tone of the neighbourhood?

Well, it's payback time.

So the next time you see your children (or better still are staying with them) it is your solemn duty to fully explore the sartorial delights of the phrase 'mutton dressed as lamb'.

(Speaking of which, have you tried getting mutton recently? Lamb you can get everywhere, but mutton is decidedly scarce. Maybe it's time to invert the phrase and start describing things as *lamb dressed as mutton*.)

You're not going out dressed like that! Some specific advice

Lycra is always a good bet. Fluorescent Lycra, ideally.

No-one likes an old fart

The term old fart is an offensive phrase usually referring to someone in authority who is set in their ways or lacking a sense of fun. I prefer a much more literal interpretation. What I propose is that you grasp the nettle and fart in public as often, and as vociferously, as possible. The chances are that the people around you will excuse your behaviour as nothing more than a symptom of some unspecified malaise associated with ageing.

What more license do you need to enjoy yourself?

Uncle Stan's Theory of Relativity

This was first expounded by my Uncle Stanley. His theory was that, relatively speaking, the older you get, the more annoying your relatives become.

Need hip replacements be so predictable?

Why not make the surgeon really earn his money? If you need a hip replaced, insist on having an elbow put in.

That'll set the tongues wagging

Ladies, feign pregnancy by shoving a pillow up your dress. Then go out with an accomplice and sit in coffee shops or restaurants and talk in a loud voice constantly dropping the name of your 'simply marvellous' Italian doctor.

'Something for the weekend, Sir?' (Or, indeed, madam)

Always keep a condom in your purse or wallet. This isn't because you have any intention of using it, but because you have every intention of letting it 'inadvertently' fall out at moments when it could cause most discomfort to your family and friends.

Just to add that extra detail that will well and truly have your children squirming with embarrassment try to make it a condom that is either 'ribbed' or 'flavoured'.

It's slang, innit

Why should impenetrable verbiage be the sole preserve of the young? A few suggestions follow.

Hip Hop
Type of dancing attempted by those who've had one or more of their hips replaced.

Ford Siesta
Nodding off in the back of a car.

Zimmered
Getting so hammered that you need support to make it home or back to your own (or ideally someone else's) bed.

God's gift
Stannah stair lift (rhyming slang).

T.P.T.
This stands for Top Plate Tango and describes
the mularkey involved in eating something
decidedly denture-unfriendly, e.g.
pomegranates.

The old how's your grandfather
Do I really have to explain this one?

Age rage
A totally justified response to encounters with
ageism.

Penile dementia
The state of confusion that grips certain men
(notably lead singers with the Rolling Stones)
who've reached an advanced age but still
believe their love interest should be young
enough to be their daughters.

Celluheavy
And you thought the cellulite of middle age was hard to face.

Wanderbra
Designed to assist ladies blessed with an ample, and once firm, bosom that now wanders off in all directions at every opportunity.

Pro-macassar
Shadowy and elusive (and historically speaking victorious) opposition to the once ubiquitous antimacassar movement.

Youthless
Apt description of attitudes and individuals that places youth at the centre of the universe.

Has it ever occurred to you just how much fun a bull can have in a China shop?

Supermarkets and department stores just love arranging their goods in eye-catching displays. And, as a child, who can say that they were never tempted to knock over a pyramid of cans? But back then you never really had the nerve to do it because you knew that you'd get 'Told Off By Your Mother'.

The question you've got to ask yourself now is: if you were 'inadvertently' to send a painstakingly arranged display tumbling, who's going to tell you off? Indeed, feign extreme regret, spiced up with a dash of doddery old fooldom, after your misdemeanour and you might even be able to blag a cup of tea out of the kindly staff whose display you've just Fred Dibnah-ed.

Strange how the horizon keeps moving further away

It is a well documented fact that old age is always ten to fifteen years older than the age that you are.

A few thoughts on built-in obsolescence (and design classics)

In a society driven by consumerism it seems that we have an insatiable desire for new things. Cars should never be more than a few years old. Fashions should change every season. And computers (for example) seem to go out of date by the time you get them out of the box and have figured out how to turn them on.

The idea of obsolescence is built-in to what we buy, and buy into, so that we can keep on consuming new stuff. Indeed so enamoured are we of consuming new stuff that things that actually do what they're supposed to, and keep on doing what they're supposed to, have to be accorded a status that elevates them above the norm. They become 'Design Classics'.

So what has all this got to do with growing older? It's simple. Things may possess built-in obsolescence, but people don't. If the society we live in thinks the opposite then it is that society itself that is obsolete. And if there is a real design classic out there, it is you and I.

That'll confuse the buggers

On a crowded bus or train, make a point of offering your seat to someone obviously much younger than yourself.

The repair man cometh

Be warned, it's a well known fact that as you get older there are dodgy repair men out there who see you as a soft touch.

If someone down the market in a brown corduroy bomber jacket tried to flog you something labelled 'The Elixir of Youth' you'd snort a snort of derision and go on your way.

Which is, of course, the exact same response you'd have to a glossy commercial on the television if someone in a white coat tried to flog you something labelled 'Anti-Ageing Cream', isn't it? (Even if it does come from the Laboratoire Ga-Ga.)

The only anti-ageing cream that really works

A huge chunk of ice cream, ideally old-fashioned vanilla, cut from a block and squidgily stuck between two flat, rectangular wafers. Eaten in the garden on the hottest day of the summer. And as it drips all over your hand and your clothes and leaks from the side of your mouth, if you don't feel like an eight year old again, then you really are beyond hope.

What's in a name?

So you hit the later years of your life and suddenly you're faced with the age-old dilemma. Namely, what name do you call yourself?

The options are bleak. There's OAP, pensioner, over 60, senior citizen, senior or wrinkly. None of them is in the least appealing as a choice. That's why over the next few pages I'd like to suggest a few alternatives.

LMA

First up is a term that derives from the practice of that oh so lovable sector of society, estate agents. When confronted with trying to flog properties in an area of a city that is less desirable than a neighbouring area they, ingeniously, reclassify the offending area as an appendage of the desirable one. Hence, in London for example, Acton is now North Chiswick. So, in the context of this book, I propose that you're no longer old, rather you're enjoying your late middle age. All of which makes you a LMA – Late Middle Ager.

Beyond Grown Updom

Next is a term that harks back to childhood's joyous optimism. Remember when you were a kid and weren't allowed to do the things you wanted to do? Everything would be different, you told yourself, when you were a Grown Up?

Well, now that you've been a Grown Up and have discovered you still weren't allowed to do the things you wanted to do, maybe you should try the nirvana of being a Grown Old.

Essentially, just as Grown Ups escape the restrictions placed on children, Grown Olds escape the restrictions placed on Grown Ups, now doesn't that sound fun.

SNDY

The third option is my favourite. It cuts to the chase and cuts through the crap.

SNDY.

Still Not Dead Yet.

You treat this place like a hotel!

Well, how else are you supposed to behave when you go round to stay with your kids? I favour complaining about the accommodation, leaving your shoes out to be polished and banging on the floor for room service whenever you fancy a snack after midnight.

And don't forget to pinch the bath robe when you go home.

Don't think of it as a stairlift, think of it as a monorail

Once again we come up against the problem of perception. So a stairlift is seen as both a badge of infirmity and as a source of sight gags for TV comedians. But look at it another way and what is a stairlift but your very own, private, monorail? And hasn't the monorail long been hailed as the perfect high-tech solution to many of the world's urban transport problems?

Key to my aim of realising the full potential of the stairlift is the quantum leap of questioning why it should be limited to only going up and down the stairs? Why can't a whole rail network of tracks serve your home? And why should they be designed to take only one passenger at a time?

Indeed if we're really going to push the envelope on stairlift design why not get the good people at Stannah to confer with rollercoaster designers from Alton Towers and come up with a track layout heavy on the wow factor. Do this and not only will you have turned the stairlift from a bit of a joke into an outstanding local visitor attraction that has kids queuing round the block, but you'll also soon be able to pay off your initial investment by charging people for the ride.

Or are you just pleased to see me?

This one's a technique for the gentlemen.

When out with friends bring the conversation around to the amazing effectiveness of Viagra. When your compatriots doubt you, produce a small tablet from your pocket and go off to find some water to take it with. While you're away remove the large courgette (or small marrow) that you've secreted in your bag or coat and arrange it appropriately in your underpants.

Return to your compatriots and apologise for the fact that sometimes the tablets don't work as well as they should.

And this one's a technique for the ladies

Visit a sex shop. Buy a vibrating egg. Take it out of its packaging and leave it lying around at home the next time your friends, neighbours, children or the vicar comes to visit.

Ask them to help you change the batteries.

How to stretch people's patience

In supermarkets pretend that you can't reach items stacked on the top shelves. Ask a customer, who is obviously in a hurry, to stretch up for you and to get them down. Then, when they give you the item, decide you don't want it and ask them (ever so sweetly) if they could put it back.

Why should New Age Travellers have all the fun?

New Age Travellers are generally frowned upon by respectable society because of the way they dress, think, don't fit in with conventions and seem to be leading a life of rootless laziness, aimlessness and fun at everyone else's expense. They're also experts at kicking up a fuss about issues to which they object.

That's why I suggest that it's high time we instigated the phenomenon of *Old* Age Travellers who would adopt a similarly admirable attitude to life.

A great way to outflank your children

Form a strategic alliance with your grandchildren. Then deploy your forces in a classic pincer movement to outmanoeuvre your enemy.

There's no statute of limitations on memories of misdemeanours

When your children have their own children, nothing causes as much irritation as undermining their authority. So when your grandchildren are old enough to understand, there's much fun to be had by regaling them with stories of all the misdemeanours that their parents got up to.

Soon you'll be safe in the knowledge that the next time your grandkids are being told off by their parents for some particular naughtiness the following lovely wail will rent the air.

'But granddad/grandma says you used to do it!'

Presents tense

There's also a great deal you can achieve by buying your grandchildren presents that their parents have sensibly refused to buy for them.

The biter bit

A set of second-hand false teeth is always a useful prop to take along to a dreaded lunch or dinner engagement. It takes but a little imagination to generate all manner of mayhem with said gnashers during the meal. My own favourite technique is to conceal the dentures in your hand, feign a coughing fit, raise your hand politely to cover the coughs, then as a particularly violent spasm grips you, fling the teeth across the room.

For added amusement try to get the teeth to land in the plate of whichever of your mealtime companions has been the most boring.

A prank to pull if you're feeling particularly mischievous

Borrow a walking stick. Go out on the streets and stand patiently by the edge of a zebra crossing. When a kindly motorist stops to let you cross, totter, painfully slowly across the road, using the walking stick as an obviously much needed support. The kindly motorist will no doubt be watching you, forced to contemplate the physical frailties that lie ahead for so many of us. Two-thirds of the way across the crossing, snatch up the walking stick and sprint the rest of the way and off into the distance. Laughing.

Welcome to your anecdotage

Entering your anecdotage can really be one of the most rewarding parts of getting older. Your aim should be to bore all those around you with stories about incidents and events that they have no interest in and, ideally, occurred long before they were born. The real skill, however, lies in selecting 'interesting' memories that are incredibly dull and 'funny' stories totally devoid of even an iota of humour, but still recounting them as if they are the most fascinating events in the history of the universe.

For added fun, invest in a stopwatch and set it going as you start your anecdote. Stop timing when you spot the first pair of eyes in your audience glazing over. Then the next time you play, try and lower your personal best time.

Aunty social behaviour

This is the overly affectionate and totally inappropriate behaviour pattern adopted in public by ageing aunts that make long since grown-up nieces and nephews cringe with embarrassment.

Please indulge in this at every possible opportunity.

A sure-fire technique for winding up your daughter or son in law

Nothing beats subtly criticising the way that your children are bringing up their children.

Existential aunts

This is a corruption of the phrase 'existential angst', though corruption may be too derogatory a word as I believe that in many ways Existential Aunts are the ultimate practitioners of existential angst.

With an Existential Aunt the philosophy of existentialism that concerns itself with the lack of any in-built meaning or purpose in the universe collides with the aunty school of behaviour in which the aunt worries unduly about how their niece or nephew is doing at school, comments on how much they've grown, and gives pathetically small gifts of money on birthdays or at Christmas.

In practice Existential Aunts say things like, 'If you're going out, make sure you wrap up warm and wear a scarf because it's freezing out there and our existence is essentially meaningless.'

As you get older remodelling yourself as an Existential Aunt provides great opportunity for both concerning and confusing your nieces and nephews.

Heart bypass

This is an admirable event that occurs later on in life when you come to the conclusion that society is increasingly unable to deal with real emotions but instead promotes overwrought sentimental tosh in their place. Prime examples of this include the over-the-top orchestrations of grief associated with national disasters, the response of spoilt brats (of all ages and political parties) when they don't get their own way, and any TV programme featuring sick animals and Rolf Harris.

A ludicrously easy way of impressing people with your vigour and vitality

Forget high energy diets. Forget rigorous exercise routines. Forget plastic surgery. Instead, when meeting new people, add fifteen years to your actual age.

Over the hill –
a re-evaluation

It's all a question of attitude. I mean, deconstruct the phrase and it reveals itself not to be so derogatory.

Climbing the hill is generally hard work. Being on top of the hill, I admit, does provide a sense of achievement and a great view. Then after that you come down the hill, which is relatively easy and enjoyable. And then you find yourself at the bottom of the hill. On a level bit.

In my experience this is where things get really interesting. And they get really interesting because you are confronted with choices. All the time you're doing all that hill work you're kind of locked into a course of action. You have to go up the hill, you have to look around at the top of it, you have to come down it. But now that you're 'over the hill' it's up to you what happens next.

Do you wander round the flat bit you're on, having fun? Do you set out in search of another hill? Do you, having done a hill, decide you'd like to have a go at a mountain? Or do you set yourself the challenge of exploring all the other geographical features that are out there? Like lakes? And rivers? And glaciers? And canyons?

Look at things this way and it soon becomes clear just how small-minded and pathetic are all those people who have the cheek to think of you, patronisingly, as being 'over the hill'. After all they're still stuck on the bloody hill. And they labour under the severely deluded misconception that the hill is all that life has to offer.

'Sing if you're glad to be grey'

At family gatherings, whenever there's a lull in the conversation, try to jolly everyone along by getting them to join in a heart warming and cheery singalong. Then choose some dire, inane, ancient ditty whose words are only known to you. However, every now and again 'forget' the words and substitute over emphatic 'la-las' and hand claps.

For added fun, whenever possible, focus your efforts on your sullen and bored teenage relatives and try to 'chivvy' them along into singing a solo.

Gullible's Travels

As retirement looms, your children will
probably start asking you what you plan to do
with all the extra time that yawns before you
like the Queen at the Cup Final. Tell them
that you've always planned to do a bit of
travelling to see a few places. Then wait till
they've exclaimed that this is a great idea and
hit them with a list of countries so troubled
that even Kate Adie would shake her head and
claim that the dog had eaten her passport.

A reintroduction to one of the long lost pleasures to be experienced in bed

For this one you have to wait until it's winter. Then wait for an evening when those bizarre oracles of meteorology with the strange hand-waving actions predict 'a heavy frost tonight'. Then turn off your central heating. Then go up to your bedroom, remove the duvet that's on the bed, and replace it with the sheet and blankets that you've invested in for this delicious saunter down Memory Lane.

Half an hour before you go to bed, boil the kettle and fill your other recent purchase – the hot water bottle. Place the hot water bottle in the bed. When it's time to retire, brush your teeth in the now freezing bathroom. Get changed in the seemingly even colder bedroom. Then climb into your bed and sink back into a sea of sensations that will have the memories flooding back.

N.B. Do make sure that you do up the stopper on the hot water bottle properly or it won't just be a sea of sensations you'll be sinking back into.

'It used to be all fields round here, you know...'

Go up to complete strangers in the street and regale them about how much things have changed 'around here' since you were a kid. Then embellish the local history lesson with spurious details about what used to be around. See how absurd you can get before your audience smells a rat.

One of the puzzling ironies associated with ageing

Even though you, as an individual, have long since stopped growing, you will find that your underwear hasn't. The older you are, the bigger it gets.

The apostrophe catastrophe

Take every opportunity to bang on at great length about how no-one today knows how to use apostrophe's correctly. Then never use them correctly yourself.

'Who's that?'

When watching even the simplest of television programs with your children constantly ask for the plot to be explained.

Game Boy

Buy a handheld electronic game console.
Make sure you've set the volume control to
maximum. Pull the game from your pocket
and start playing it at the most inappropriate
moments. For example, while you're in
church. Or during a trip to the theatre. Or
while your partner is trying to have a
conversation with you.

Game Boy – advanced

Or while your partner is trying to make love
to you.

Throwing a spaniel in the works

At Christmas buy your grandchildren a puppy. Having made certain not to clear it with their parents first. And if you do have more than one grandchild it's probably best that they get one puppy each. After all, it's only fair.

The last wish letter

The concept here is very simple. All you have to do is to perfect the art of writing the 'last wish' letter. In the letter you claim to be suffering from something tragic and incurable. Then say that there's one thing you've always dreamt of doing. It might be sitting in a box at the opera, having a weekend at the Ritz, or going on a flight in a hot air balloon. What's more, now that time is running out, you really want to give it a try.

Now here's the subtle bit, offer to pay for said adventure with money that you've saved up from your pension. Then send the letter off to the relevant people.

Write the letters well enough and I reckon about fifty percent of the people you target should come up with the goods for free.

Ashes to ashes

Invest in a small urn. Fill it with the ashes of some disposable item you've burnt on a bonfire. Then the next time unsuspecting friends, relatives or neighbours visit your home, position the urn in such a place that they will inevitably knock it over and spill the contents while you are out of the room. Then sit back and enjoy the show.

More ashes to ashes

Again invest in a small urn. Again fill it with ashes. Then dress up in your best dark suit and take the urn, and the ashes, out with you to scatter them in their final resting place.
Choose a location and a time that are highly inappropriate. For example, on the platform of a busy station in the middle of the morning rush hour. Or in a churchyard just as a photographer is arranging the group picture of a wedding. Or in your neighbours' back garden when they're having a barbecue.

Digging up the hatchet

Over the course of your life you have probably been involved in many disputes. They may have been over work, or love, or family matters or any number of other things. Being the sensible person that you are, you no doubt realised that if a satisfactory resolution wasn't to be had the best thing to do would be to let the matter go and get on with your life.

Well, now's the time to jettison all that namby-pamby, forgive and forget nonsense and sort the matter out once and for all. And if you don't fancy the prospect of a confrontation in person, then just send a letter with the simple, reassuring, unsigned message 'I haven't forgiven you.'

Then you can move on. And you'll be safe in the knowledge that your old adversary will have to, at the very least, spend some time contemplating all the people they've stitched up in their life.

After all, don't the Sicilians say that 'Revenge is a dish best served cold.' (Which makes revenge a dish very similar to gazpacho.)

A great way to get free food

Before any member of your family or any of
your friends come round to visit take all the
food out of your fridge and hide it somewhere.
Leave only a half eaten small tin of beans, a
souring carton of milk and a hardened crust of
bread. Then contrive a circumstance that has
your visitor opening your fridge. Also suck
your cheeks in, try to look 'peeky' and feign
weariness throughout the visit.

Briefs encounter

Passion doesn't disappear as the years pass. It's more that its nature changes. Also that the opportunities to act upon the impulses that seize us have to battle against the inertia of habit and convention. And all too often fear of what others will think acts as the most over-zealous of chaperones.

Which is a shame, because in the words of the old song, 'A little of what you fancy does you good'.

But be warned because when you do carpe the diem, and succumb to the delights of a blood-pumpingly passionate bit of groping and grappling, there will come the Briefs Encounter Moment. This is the moment when you're stopped in your tracks by the sobering thought that if things do go any further you will have to reveal the full horror, scope, scale and general demeanour of the underwear that you are wearing.

The wisdom of the ancients

One of the benefits of getting older is that for some obscure reason there lingers around the peripheries of most societies the quasi-folkloric idea that the old can be very wise. Frankly, this is too good an opportunity to miss. That's because it provides you with a licence to talk cobblers, dressed up in profundity.

To help you with this exercise I've put down a few suggestions of my own. But the most fun is to be had by making the things up for yourself.

The wisdom of the ancients – a few examples

1. It is easier for a rich man to needle a camel by poking him in the eye, than it is for a fat man to get into the Kingdom of Leather.

2. If trees were made of cheese, then owls would live in Gouda.

3. Where there's muck, there's someone who's really let their standards slip.

4. If the fire wasn't hot how on earth would we cook the porridge?

5. The movement you want is on your shoulder.

(OK, so I admit I didn't make that last one up, but nicked it from 'Hey Jude'. But I've always had no idea what it means. So I thought I'd stick it in on the off chance that Sir Paul would read it and get in touch.)

You're not getting old, you're investigating Chaos Theory

Chaos Theory is one of the real hot potatoes in the world of super-intellectual, ivory-towered boffins who rack their brains and run the world's megacomputers ragged trying to explain the true nature of the cosmos. Chaos Theory states that even the most basic rules can occasionally behave in totally unpredictable ways.

So when one morning you get up and find that the simple task of getting dressed has suddenly become complicated due to creaking limbs, aching joints or failing eyesight, don't put it down to ageing. Put it down to Chaos Theory.

Indeed, put together a decent proposal and you might even be able to con some cash out of the government so that you can further your researches.

An easy way to say 'hi' to the passing world

Eschew conventional pot plants like geraniums and busy lizzies when deciding what to place in your windows. Instead cultivate real pot plants. Marijuana is both decorative and useful. And should the local constabulary query your horticultural selections, explain that you are merely making early preparations for the onset of arthritis in an attempt to ease the financial burden on the overstretched NHS.

Banging On

Banging On is one of the true pleasures of attaining a venerable age. It is a skill that is easily achieved and that is infinitely adaptable to almost any set of circumstances. What you need to do is find a topic that you know very little about, then talk about it for as long as possible.

Indeed in the ideal Banging On scenario the amount of knowledge possessed should be in precise inverse proportion to the length of conversation attempted. And now that I come to think of it, 'conversation' is the wrong word. A well-honed Banging On session should at all times attempt to become a monologue. And better still, a monologue that wears the demeanour of a lecture.

Probably the best setting for Banging On is a long car journey.

Something to chew over

Much fun can be had by always offering wine
gums to friends with false teeth.

Coffee shop fun

Look, it's their own fault. I mean you go into
a coffee shop wanting a simple cup of coffee
and suddenly you're confronted with more
choices than the Pope on an official visit to
Denmark where a rather over-elaborate
smorgasbord has been laid on for lunch.

Well, this is how you can get your own
back.

What you do is peer up at the long list of
coffee options so proudly proclaimed on the
signage on the wall and, one by one, ask what
they are. At the end of each description say
'Oh, that sounds nice', pause as if you're
about to order what's just been described,
then apologetically ask about the next coffee
on the list.

Carry on until all the coffees have been described, then throw the whole situation back in the lap of the counter staff by feigning confusion and asking them what they think you should have.

Ponder their suggestion for a minute, then with a mildly triumphant little sigh say 'I know, I'll have a nice cup of tea.'

Game, set and match to you, I think.

The best way to help your children avoid inheritance tax

Spend all the money before you pop your clogs.

And you thought mobile phones were a pain in the bum

Get yourself a mobile phone. But make sure it's got a hands-free kit with it. Then put it away in a cupboard until you need it. And when you need it will be that fateful day when you discover that you've started to talk to yourself in public.

Under these circumstances, retrieve your phone, fit the earpiece, and hit the streets. Now you can be secure in the knowledge that no-one will suspect that you're talking to yourself – they'll just think that you're 'on your mobile'.

The problem with Zimmer frames

Look, I realise that the prospect of Zimmerdom is probably off in the dim and distant but I think that's precisely why we should consider the blighters now. That way we can turn the Zimmer frame from an object of ridicule into a much sought after lifestyle statement as coveted as the latest Fendi bag or Apple Macintosh laptop.

Up until now Zimmer frames have been thought of only in functional terms. Their design was purely utilitarian.

Hence the current Zimmer frame looks like nothing more than a very basic scaffolding construction which, while setting the Zimmeree free mobility-wise, also, and somewhat ironically, imprisons them in a perceptual cage of infirmity.

Clearly what's needed is a radical re-imagination of the damned thing.

I mean, what would a Zimmer frame designed by Phillipe Starck look like? Or one that had been subject to the magical eye of John Galliano? Or what about Damien Hirst? What would a Damien Hirst Zimmer frame look like? Now wouldn't that have all the Sunday papers clamouring to get the 'New Zimmers' on the front of their magazines?

So in this brave new world the Zimmer frame would not be stigmatised, but would be the subject of waiting lists at the most exclusive of boutiques. And potential purchasers would have to prove their infirmity even to get in to see the latest Zimmer frame collections from Paris and Milan.

'Regrets, I've had a few'

Who's Frank kidding? We've all got regrets.
Loads of the buggers. And if we really think
we've got 'too few to mention' it's more likely
a case that we can't remember all the stupid
things we've done in our life, or all the bad
decisions we've made.

After all, wasn't it the French existentialist
Albert Camus who wrote (in French
obviously) 'A man without regrets is like a
grapefruit without a grapefruit knife'?

Anyway, my point is that the only thing
worth really regretting is having no regrets.
Indeed, it is my profound belief that regrets
should be got out and agonised over at regular
intervals. That's because regrets can help give a
patina of depth to your life. They enable you
to say to yourself, 'Look, I'm not a shallow

person because in my life I've made bad decisions and suffered because of them.'

And it's vitally important that you share these regrets with your nearest and dearest as frequently as possible. Boy, will that wind them up.

A couple of examples follow.

I should have married someone else

This is a cracking regret to throw into the mix at the appropriate moment. It conjures up images of long-lost love, long-suffering marriage and the worrying implication that your children are somehow not quite up to scratch.

I was a real high-flyer

Primarily a tactic to be employed by the older woman. The essence of it is that you gave up a more than promising career in order to look after your kids. To add a real subtle twist of the knife to this ploy, whenever the subject comes up, look a little wistful and say in a soft voice, 'No, of course I don't regret it.'

That's guaranteed to generate guilt trips of the highest order in your children. What bliss.

It's not the silence of the lambs that's the real horror story, it's the groaning of the limbs

So you used to spring out of bed every morning, but now you're more likely to wake having felt every spring. Unfortunately aching limbs come with the territory of age. Of course, there are various sensible things you can do to ease the situation. You can change your diet. You can start exercising. You can buy a new bed. Or you can initiate an illicit affair with someone totally inappropriate so that every morning you're too busy making love, or too racked with guilt, to notice your aching limbs.

Not that hard a decision, is it?

Twist and shout

Buy two jars of some everyday foodstuff.
Remove the lid from one jar. Superglue the
rim. Replace the lid. Leave the glue to harden.
Then the next time a friend or relative comes
to visit, feign aged feebleness, and ask them to
help you open the jar with the glued lid.
Watch expectantly as they puff, pant and
strain. Then intervene saying that you'll
return it to the shop. Take the jar back to the
kitchen, switch with the undoctored one,
return to your friend or relative and suggest
you'll have one last try to open the jar. Then
open the jar easily.

As a stylish finishing touch, thank your
friend or relative for their help and let them
go on their way.

The age of enlightenment or the age for a light enema?

One of the most perplexing things you can do as far as your children are concerned is to embrace the pleasures of alternative medicine. Which is why it's a great wheeze to pretend that you have. The dodgier the treatment you purport to be indulging in, the better. You know the kind of thing – jojoba and tofu body rubs, boll weevil extract dietary supplements, and any exercise regime that involves you standing in the garden in the early morning wearing only your underpants.

The Holy Grail of all this misleading of your offspring is to convince them of the benefits of colonic irrigation to such an extent that they try it for themselves. Especially if you've never actually had a Dyson shoved up your nether regions yourself. What fun.

Generation Vex

This is a phrase derived from the 1990s term Generation X describing a generation of young people disaffected, directionless and having no part to play in society. It's a situation with which many older people can identify.

Generation Vex is a response to this disagreeable state of affairs. As in you don't have to sit there and just accept the role society has mapped out for you. You can complain. And you should complain. Especially when you find yourself defined and delimited by other people's preconceived ideas of what age means.

Last chance for a mid-life crisis

If you didn't have one during your mid-life (traditionally when you hit 40) then it really is about time you had one now. If you don't then you will have missed out on one of life's great opportunities to create stress and concern for those who really care about you. And you will also have missed out on the licence to behave badly that is usually extended to those enjoying a mid-life crisis.

In its classic manifestation a mid-life crisis revolves around the realisation that the career that you've invested so much time and effort in is in the doldrums and no longer satisfying, as is (or so you imagine) your marriage, and your relationship with your children. So you look around for some totally inappropriate way in which to rebel.

Described in these terms it's easy to see why hitting 60 plus and realising that you haven't had a mid-life crisis is rather like finding an old premium bond in a drawer that has long ago won a prize that you can still claim.

Typical options for Late-Mid-Life-Crisis-induced bad behaviour include having an affair with someone much younger, 'investing' in plastic surgery, buying a Harley Davidson, and opting out of all the choices and beliefs and obligations that once delimited your life.

Now if you can't have fun with those as your starter for ten, then you're not really trying.

The joy of slacks

There will come a point in your life when the wearing of slacks will start to appeal much more. Embrace the moment and incorporate the philosophy implicit in the name of that garment into your lifestyle. 'Slacks' derives from 'slack', a word meaning 'not tight, taut, tense, or busy'. What a great way to live.

The wine and cheese analogy of ageing

Wine improves with age. As does cheese. But both have to be stored in a cool place to do so. In many ways we possess similar qualities to both cheese and wine. That's why heading off somewhere hot and sunny to spend your retirement may not have the hoped-for effect.

After all, while a ripe camembert may be a thing of beauty, one that's completely melted in the heat and run off down the cheeseboard, down the legs of the dining table and out into the night in search of a cab isn't the sort of thing you want to be confronted by every time you look in the bathroom mirror.

A very good reason to wear too much make-up

It'll really embarrass your children.

A whole new approach to the Seven Deadly Sins

1. Sloth
2. Avarice
3. Envy
4. Lust
5. Anger
6. Gluttony
7. Pride

Think of it as a checklist of things to do.

'He's in his shed'

Incidentally, that last piece on drugs lends a whole new dimension to the attractions of a 'potting' shed.

Queue jumping

It's really annoying when some cocky oik of a youth arrogantly shoves their way to the front of the queue where you, and others, have been queuing patiently. Unsurprisingly, it's just as annoying if you, as someone old enough to know better, did the same. So lose your inhibitions and give it a go.

'We're all going on a summer holiday ...'

No more worries for a week or two? Oh really?

Never underestimate the fun to be had by going on holiday with your children's family. After all, on what other occasion would you find yourself with so many new places, experiences and things to complain about?

And you don't even have to wait to get to your holiday destination to get the stress-inducing ball rolling. For example, if you're flying you can insist on getting to the airport a good hour and a half before check-in time 'just to be on the safe side'. Or if you're travelling by car, 'Are we there yet?' is too irritating a question just to be left to your grandchildren.

When you do get to wherever you're staying, in response to the inevitable question 'Do you like it?' pause just long enough to plant a seed of doubt then say 'It's very nice.' But subsequently drop subtle hints that you're not over keen on the room, the view, the other holidaymakers, the locals, the weather and indeed the country you're visiting.

Then go on a vain hunt for a 'decent cup of tea'. And report back with your findings. It's also worthwhile forgetting to take along a book to read and then borrowing the one brought by your son- or daughter-in-law. But for added spice remember to take along a copy of the weekly TV guide from home. And every evening regale your companions with all your 'favourite' programmes that you're missing by being away.

Then on your last night get completely plastered on some vile-tasting liqueur and end up snogging someone you shouldn't on the dance floor of the local disco, leaving your kids to drag you off saying, 'If we don't go now we'll miss the plane!'

After all, isn't that what you had to do with them all those years ago?

The gap year

This is another concept wasted on the young.
Essentially it's a year out between finishing
school and going on to college or university.
The idea is that the callow youth in question
broadens their horizons, sees a bit of the
world, gains some independence and lets their
hair down before they get mired in the serious
business of study. It should also involve much
drinking, carousing and inappropriate sexual
shenanigans. (Just so long as the parents don't
find out.)

Which is all well and good but why should
this Gap Year thing (which in my day was
either not an option or had the slightly
different name of 'arseing about') be only
available to the young who have, frankly, done
very little to deserve it? That's why I propose

that in between the day you retire and the day you actually start your retirement, you too should be entitled to head off on a Gap Year.

The idea is that the not-so-callow individual in question broadens their horizons, sees a bit of the world, gains some independence and lets what's left of their hair down before they get mired in the serious business of retirement. It should also involve much drinking, carousing and inappropriate sexual shenanigans. (Just so long as the children don't find out.)

Is it just me, or is small print getting smaller?

No, it's not getting smaller. So stop being so vain and get yourself some decent glasses.

Been there, done that, got the T-shirt

This is a conversational ploy that is particularly effective in annoying anyone younger than yourself. Whenever said younger person is talking about any particular experience that they've recently experienced, good, bad, or indifferent, hit them with this phrase.

By doing so you will be letting them know, not too subtly, that whatever they've done, enjoyed or lived through, you did it all first and, hence, their experiences are in no way original and, double hence, somehow less valid and, triple hence, their life is about as interesting as a repeat of *Crossroads*.

A trip down mammary lane (for the ladies)

This involves a stint in front of the mirror lamenting how it's not only governments with large majorities that seem to lose shape, firmness and direction as time goes on.

A trip down mammary lane (for the gentlemen)

This involves a walk outside on a hot summer's day when, in the words of the old song 'June is busting out all over' and so are all her mates. And the realisation strikes you that you've completely forgotten what a certain part of the opposite sex's anatomy feels like.

Wrinklies: how to reclaim, redefine and defuse abuse

Some people think that the best way to deal with verbal abuse is to rise above it. My preferred approach is to undermine it. Just like Cyrano de Bergerac did that time when someone foolishly mocked his big nose. So if the term 'wrinkly' does come your way throw it straight back and suggest one of the following self-deprecating, yet self-empowering alternatives instead.

Shrinkly An older person who finds themselves somewhat diminished in stature

Thinkly   Anyone over 60 who spends a lot of time thinking about profound and important stuff

Sprinkly Any compatriot afflicted by incontinence

Crinkly Old, but in the delightful position of being in possession of lots of the folding stuff

Drinkly Those who indulge in the occasional tipple at every possible opportunity

Pinkly An individual who still holds to a left-wing or Marxist analysis of life

Pinkly Alternatively, someone both grey and gay

Winkly People who see no reason why age should be a barrier to flirting

Kinkly People who see no reason why age should be a barrier to a, let's just say, 'imaginative' approach to sex

Nodding off

Now this is one of the true delights to be had in the Gorgeous Garden of Getting On. Basically, you're allowed to nod off. So whenever, for example, you're bored out of your skull by the mindless inanity of the conversation your family is pursuing round the table after Sunday lunch, just drop your chin on to your chest, let your eyelids droop, and pretend to fall asleep.

Your family, bless them, will think that you're 'tired'. But little will they suspect that what you're really tired of is them.

In one end, out the other. Or not, as the case may be

Bowel problems are another great aspect of getting older that can be fruitfully discussed at family gatherings. In a loud voice. At meal times.

'Are you looking at me?' (as Robert De Niro once so succinctly put it)

Get together with a group of fellow compatriots of a similar age as yourself and hang around on street corners smoking cigarettes and kicking an empty lager can about. Don't move aside when anyone under the age of twenty tries to get past. For added menace turn up the collar on your anorak. (And turn down the volume on your hearing aid.)

Remember the days when Bobby Charlton was famous for being a footballer?

For gentlemen most of whose hair has long since decided it's time to vacate headquarters, the most sensible option is to wear what's left in a short, well-groomed arrangement. Growing it long and then brushing it sideways, or indeed forwards, in a vain attempt to cover up an otherwise bald pate fools no-one and can only result in furtive hilarity among all those who see it. For this reason it is imperative that you adopt the Bobby Barnet at the earliest possible opportunity. Think of it less as a hairstyle, and more as a chance to spread a little light relief among the youthful masses who lead such dull and dreary lives that they're desperate for even the smallest diversion to smile about.

Home alone? Then why not home a loan?

In the movie *Home Alone* the child actor Macauley Culkin, left behind (accidentally) by his parents, thwarts a bunch of adult burglars intent on stripping his home of all its valuable assets.

To the unenlightened viewer it is nothing more than a lightweight bit of slapstick fun. But take a more philosophical stance and what is revealed is a far profounder critique of the way society treats the disenfranchised.

Recast Macauley's role as that of an older person, left behind not by his parents but his adult children, then re-imagine these adult children as the burglars and *Home Alone* becomes a searing indictment of the way that your children abandon you in a house you worked all your life to buy, then can't wait for you to pop your clogs so that they can sell the place and make a killing.

But the true genius of *Home Alone* is in its title. A title that suggests a solution to the predicament. Namely take a loan out against the value of your home, and blow the cash before your offspring can get their mitts on it.

And that's why *Home Alone* is a masterpiece and a far better and more relevant analysis of ageing than even *King Lear*.

'Language, Timothy!'

It is a well known fact that certain age-related disorders have the disconcerting side effect of loosening the constraints of polite behaviour. One of the prime manifestations of this is the sudden appearance of foul and abusive language in the mouths of the gentlest of souls.

Now if that doesn't sound like a worthwhile condition to fake, then you're not really entering into the spirit of the whole 'Growing Old Disgracefully' philosophy.

We rejected the Nanny State, shouldn't we do the same for the Granny State?

The Granny State presupposes that anyone who is a grandmother has to act in certain, granny-like ways. They must have kindly faces and outlooks, they must knit and wear cardigans, and they must be mildly shocked at the goings-on of youngsters. And, of course, they must never have sex. Or even think about it.

What rubbish.

A few alternative granny role models follow.

E.G.

This stands for Essex Granny. Let's just say she is a female contemporary who's old enough to know better, dress better and act better. The Essex Granny wears dresses that are cut too low, heels that are way too high and, of an evening out, has aims and tactics that are decidedly below the belt. Hence she is a fantastic role model for growing old disgracefully.

Ethics Granny

At the other end of the spectrum of grannydom from the Essex Granny is the Ethics Granny.

The Ethics Granny objects to everything. For ethical reasons. Ethical reasons that she expounds loud and clear at every possible opportunity. Especially when in the company of her children.

The Tranny Granny

This is an approach for the more adventurous-minded woman. Basically you decide late on in the game that cross-dressing is the lifestyle option that you feel most comfortable with. Give no word of warning, nor explanation, just turn up one day at your children's house dressed as a man.

That should set the cat among the canaries.

The Fanny Granny

No, it's not what you think.

    This is a granny who spreads mild annoyance and minor irritation by fannying around all the time. Key phrases to be used include 'Now where did I put my glasses?', 'Oooh, did I leave the light on in the hall?' and 'Now tell me dear, which part of my body do you think I should get pierced next?'

The Canny Granny

By far the best category of granny. The original role model hails from Newcastle. They boast a similar attitude to life as the Essex Granny, but with a better dress sense. And a more direct approach to the things they want. As in 'Grab yer coat toy boy, yer've pulled an owld lass.'

Birds do it, bees do it (even creaking OAPs do it)

Sex is another one of those things that's too much fun to be left to the young. And just because a lot of water may have passed under several of your bridges doesn't mean you can't still have a fair bit of fun splashing around in a boat, if you catch my drift.

What follows are just a few suggestions.

Consult the Calmer Sutra

This is a collection of sexual positions from the East devised for those who, in matters connected with jiggery pokery, are still interested in the pokery side of things but find that they need to cut down on the jiggery end of it all.

Positions featured include The Dromedary (one hump), The Tethered Zimmer (light bondage), The Drooping Palm (don't worry, it happens to everyone) and The Gushing Well (far too rude to even attempt to explain).

Dressing up

One of the commonest fantasies. For the older man the fantasy usually involves having their partners dress up as St Trinian's style schoolgirls, or nurses, or Charlie Dimmock on a rainy day. (Like that's ever going to happen.)

For the older woman the fantasy usually involves having their partner dress up in a clean pair of unbaggy Y-fronts. (Like that's ever going to happen.)

Another common fantasy

Another common fantasy for men of a certain age and social background involves the wearing of stockings, suspenders and high heel shoes. But hey, ladies, as long as they don't put ladders in your stockings or break the heels of your shoes my advice is why not let your partners wear the stuff? Indeed, encourage them to pursue their 'hobby' and it's a great way of increasing your wardrobe.

Rubberware

Now here's a fetish that we really should encourage older people to get into. After all, there is a potential dual benefit. First, there's sexual gratification. Secondly, if incontinence ever does become a problem in later life, you're ahead of the game in terms of clothing.

Strip teas

For this you need cucumber sandwiches, scones, strawberry jam and a pot of Earl Grey. You also need to invite someone over for tea. Then as the comestibles are consumed you gradually remove your clothing. How far you go and what you get up to are entirely up to you.

But don't forget, always warm the pot first.

Cream teas

Like strip teas, but a far squidgier encounter.

HRTs

Similar to strip teas and cream teas, but with a renewed zest for life, re-invigorated hair and a glowing complexion.

Hee-haw, ha-ha

Let it be known to your nearest and dearest that (being of sound mind and body) you're giving serious consideration to the matter of your will. Then casually leave lying around brochures for a donkey sanctuary.

'It's the brand new geegaw, that can access the whatsit and has shedloads of thingummy'

If new technology makes you feel stupid, then you're missing the point. That's because the point of new technology is to make you feel stupid. That way the manufacturers know that when the next new technology arrives you'll probably buy that too, in the vain hope that it's easier to understand.

But, for the older person, there is an upside to this madness. This is the fact that while you may find it hard to get to grips with the intricacies of the new technologies, so do your children. But seeing as they are much younger than you, and kid themselves that they are at one with this rapidly changing world, they will feel that they should understand it all.

So invest in the latest geegaw, get everything out of the box and jumble it up a bit, then take it round to your son or son-in-law's place and ask them to help you sort it out. Then sit back and enjoy the show.

You should be in line for at least a good couple of hours' entertainment. Plus the ten minutes at the end when your grandson or granddaughter gets back from school and sets it all up without even looking at the instructions.

A Proustian interlude

Proust, in his magnum opus *A la recherche du temps perdu*, apparently only had to taste a Madeleine and all kinds of memories came flooding back from earlier years. When I first heard this I quickly sought out the book only to be sorely disappointed to discover that the Madeleine in question was a cake and not a character.

But Proust was making a very good point. The taste of something from our childhood or youth can easily reveal a room full of memories. So what is your equivalent of Proust's Madeleines?

Is it the tinned salmon you used to eat at your auntie's house for Sunday tea? Or the tongue-blackening delights of a quarter of liquorice allsorts? Or is it the spam fritters they used to serve every Thursday at school?

The thing to do is track them down and try them. And see what memories come flooding back.

Then again there is always the possibility that the taste that you most long for is the taste of a Madeleine. Or a Margaret. Or a Michael. Or a Malcolm. In which case re-creating the sensation might be somewhat harder to achieve.

The caterpillar theory

Everyone knows that people are living longer, healthier lives these days. Yet at the same time everyone seems to accept the fact that society has inexorably shifted its focus and its centre of power from the old to the young. This makes no sense at all.

If you want an analogy from the world of nature it's as if caterpillars were to suddenly adopt the ethos that being a caterpillar was the be all, and end all, of everything. Hence the retreat into a cocoon and the subsequent emergence with wings must come as quite a considerable shock. Indeed so great a surprise is it that they may well spend their time crawling around still trying to be caterpillars. Which is rather stupid.

After all, the best thing to do with a pair of wings is to take to the air and fly.

Another biting comment

It's always worth remembering that everyone you meet will, at some point in the encounter, benefit from you sharing with them:

a. Your age.

b. The fact that you've got all your own teeth.

Nostalgia isn't what it used to be

Nostalgia was so much better in the old days. But now it's almost a case of last month's hype being this month's nostalgia. What the concept of nostalgia needs is a good kick up the backside.

Some new categories would be a good starting point.

Nicestalgia

This involves sitting around, drinking tea and eating cakes, discussing how much nicer everything was way back when everyone thought Lapsang Souchong was the exiled leader of Tibet and Mr Kipling, not Jane Asher, was the top banana of cakery.

Knowstalgia

A trusty standby of a rant that essentially bemoans the fact that since they've stopped using slide rules and log tables in schools no-one seems to know very much at all, about anything, and especially about grammar and speling.

Noosestalgia

A practice to be saved for the occasions when trapped in a social situation with anyone who wears their oh-so-pious left-wing conscience on their sleeve like a macaroon. The basic line you should adopt is that there was much less crime about when, every now and again, someone got hanged.

Knorrstalgia

A light soufflé of a discussion centred on the fact that food tasted so much better in the old days when there were far fewer ingredients to choose from and instead of things like balsamic vinegar you made do with that bog standard, industrial strength, brown stuff that made a bag of chips reek like a kipper factory, but taste like heaven, and the height of sophistication in the kitchen was the humble stock cube.

Nursestalgia

This is a train of thought that you will catch in your much later years when you find yourself sat up in bed on the receiving end of a particularly brusque bed-bath from a rather hefty-looking nurse who would obviously rather be doing something else. I mean, wasn't it supposed to be like that scene with Joanne Whalley in The Singing Detective?

Soixante-neufstalgia

This is a sordid and rather grubby form of nostalgia and I'm surprised at you for reading about it. It encompasses the erotic reverie that engulfs you when you get to pondering on just how much fun you had during your sexual canoodlings of yesteryear.

How to keep your partner on their toes

Take a new interest in your appearance. Buy and wear a new perfume or aftershave. Start going out a lot on your own for no apparent reason. Pretend to be happy.

But the age of romance needn't be dead – not when the romance of age can still burn bright

If you are in the fortunate position of still being with someone you love, then copy out the following and post it to them in a letter. Don't wait until it's too late to tell them what you feel. It's from Shakespeare's Sonnets. And how wrong can you go with a Shakespeare sonnet?

> To me, fair friend, you never can be old,
> For as you were when first your eye I ey'd,
> Such seems your beauty still.

Three rather surprising but quite amusing things to try with your bus pass

1. Jimmying open the lock of someone's car.

2. Trying to get an extra discount on crockery or clothing on the first day of the Harrods sale.

3. Chopping up a line of talcum powder on a small mirror and offering it round as cocaine the next time those nicely turned out young Americans who've witnessed Jehovah come round trying to save your soul.

It's amazing the things you can find shoved down the back of the closet

One of the most disquieting revelations that you can spring on your family is the fact that for most of your adult life you've suspected that you were gay. (Or, as the case may be, straight.) Such is the potency of this tactic that it really should only be deployed under specific, sensitive and easily controlled circumstances. Personally I recommend Christmas lunch, just before the turkey is carved.

That'll put a whole new twist on listening to the Queen's speech.

Aged provocateur

There are establishments in London's Soho that purvey all manner of saucy lingerie to a discerning and playful clientele. Lace, frills and straps all feature prominently. As does a gorgeously salacious touch of sleaze. Now if you're of the opinion that your days of even considering such accoutrements, let alone wearing them, are way behind you, think again.

After all, just because the present may have seen better days doesn't mean the wrapping paper can't still be fab. And what better way to signal to both yourself and your partner that sex is too much fun just to be left to the young. Indeed, even if you don't want to get into all the gloriously grubby sordidness that jiggery-pokery often involves, it's still worth buying a little something just to leave lying around inadvertently the next time your children come over for a visit.

Nothing annoys like the noise of toys

When your children's children stop being babies they'll love nothing more than playing with toys that make a noise. And the noisier the noise, the better. Naturally drums are a big hit, as are all manner of playthings that emit ear-piercing shrieks and wails or mind-numbing nursery rhyme tunes. Unsurprisingly this behaviour will drive their parents mad.

All of which really simplifies buying presents for your grandchildren come Christmas or on birthdays.

'How could you say that?'

When round at your children's place having a meal with their friends it's always worthwhile dropping into any lull in the conversation an embarrassing anecdote about their behaviour when they were little. Indeed the memory doesn't even have to be accurate, as you can always deny any denial they make by adding, 'Well, you probably don't remember.'

For example, 'Oh, my little Johnny used to play with himself all the time when he was little' is always a winner.

Life in the slow lane

Whenever you get in your car, wherever you're going, drive really slowly. When driving on a motorway, drive in the outside lane and stick to the speed limit. After all, it is the law.

Life in the slow lane. Two

Always remember to do your shopping on a Saturday. Use only the biggest of trolleys available. Place two, or at most three, small items in the trolley. Then endeavour to block each aisle in turn by moving along it as slowly as possible, carefully scrutinising the serried ranks of goods on offer as you go. Every now and again suddenly stop your perambulations and pick up some item for closer inspection. Also wander away from your trolley frequently, ideally leaving it at right angles to the shelves. The busy intersections of aisles are also excellent places to position your trolley to generate the maximum inconvenience. With but a little practice you should be able to pass a whole afternoon enjoyably in this way.

Why wait to lose your marbles when so much fun can be had by pretending to misplace them every now and again?

Need I say more?

Dad, it's me ...

Much fun can be had by writing to your male contemporaries and claiming to be the now grown up son or daughter they unknowingly fathered over thirty years ago.

Too many cooks

Next time you're round visiting your children's home for a meal, offer to help with the cooking. Once your offer has been accepted there are many, many ways to have fun.

There's the 'Oh, I thought you hadn't put the salt in yet' technique; the 'Sorry, I thought it was on too high/too low' approach; and finally, the *pièce de résistance* that will truly brûlé their crèmes: 'That's not the way to do it. Here, let me show you.'

Drive them potty

Another winning technique for use when round your children's house for a meal.

After everyone's eaten, offer to help with the washing up. Then once everything is washed, put all the pots and pans and plates and dishes carefully away. In the wrong places.

The beauty of this tactic is that you'll be long gone from the scene of the crime when the irritation really kicks in.

Sweets: the bitter truth

All your grandchildren love you buying sweets, chocolates or ice-creams for them. But their parents would much prefer it if you didn't. Especially if you hand over said goodies just before mealtimes.

Act accordingly.

Cats 22

You'd have to be mad to want to live in a house with 22 cats. But if you did, then all kinds of fools would not bother knocking on your door. Like canvassing politicians, or oafs selling cleaning products, or those nicely suited shysters wondering if you're happy with your gas supplier. You know, all those people with irritating sales pitches designed to drive you mad.

What I'm getting at is that maybe the best way to preserve your sanity is to occasionally feign a little madness. For instance, by living in a house with 22 cats.

Congratulations! You're a grandad/grandmother

A funny thing happens when your kids have kids. Suddenly you'll find yourself incredibly popular. Now it may well be because your children want you to share in the joy of their family life. Or it may be because they want a cheap babysitter.

You decide.

And while we're on the subject of babysitting

Of course, there are other reasons that you're popular as a babysitter for your grandchildren apart from the issue of cost. In the eyes of your children, unlike conventional babysitters, you're unlikely to raid the drinks cupboard, run up massive phone bills or bonk your boyfriend on the sofa.

Which is all the more reason why you should do all three.

Deafinitely a winner

When out shopping pretend to be deaf. Keep repeating 'Sorry?' and 'You'll have to speak up.' Eventually the unfortunate trying to communicate with you will end up bawling their head off just to get you to understand them. At this point affect a look of shock and rebuke them with the phrase, 'You don't have to shout, I'm not deaf!'

E. W. B.

There are many pivotal moments in history
that divide the world into one state of affairs
before the moment, and a significantly
different one after it. For example, there's the
moment when women first got the vote. Or
the moment when Neil Armstrong first
stepped on the moon. Or the moment when
the Berlin Wall came down.

For the older person, sartorially speaking,
there is a moment just as significant. That's
the moment when the desire for comfort
overrides the desire to look fashionable and
you realise that Elasticated Waist Bands aren't
such a bad idea after all.

Christmas or Christmiss?

As you get older your nearest and dearest will no doubt find it incumbent upon them to invite you around at Christmas. They could, of course, be doing this out of love and affection. However they are much more likely to be doing it out of guilt. They can't bear the thought of you being alone at Christmas. Or, more accurately, they can't bear the thought of what people will think if they let you be alone at Christmas. So they invite you over.

The truly objectionable thing is that you're supposed to be grateful. Grateful that you have to spend time in a house full of screaming kids. Grateful that you can't watch any of the TV programmes you've been looking forward to seeing. Grateful for a lunch served so late that it's almost supper. Grateful for having to eat Brussels sprouts just to set your grandchildren an example. Grateful for another pair of socks or another gift-pack of nauseatingly pongy bath stuff. And grateful for being forced to confront just what a disappointing bunch of reprobates your family turned out to be.

My advice would be to feign illness. And make it something terribly infectious. Then phone through to your loved ones a list of the requirements you'll need while you're confined to your home saying, in a rather pathetic voice, that 'you haven't been able to make it to the shops'. And to really pile on the guilt add the phrase, 'But don't worry about me, I'll be alright.'

New from the makers of Viagra

Seeing as Viagra has been such a hit maybe it's about time the manufacturers broadened their horizons?

Shyagra   For those who find themselves increasingly unwilling to meet new people as they get older

Tryagra   For those who become unwilling to try new things as they age

Dryagra   For those suffering from incontinence

Whyagra   For people unwilling to ask questions, especially of those in authority, e.g. doctors

Fryagra A truly remarkable drug that enables those with high blood pressure, heart problems or cholesterol build-up to eat fried foods including the glorious full English breakfast

Whyohwhyohwhyagra For people who spend all their time asking questions on programmes like *Points of View* or Radio Four's *Feedback*

Niagra For those having difficulty passing water

Piagra For those who find it difficult, even under the most favourable of circumstances, to divide the circumference of a circle by its diameter

Byebyeagra For those who can't face the prospect of going to another funeral

This Be The Verse (Only Much Later On)

They muck you up, your son and daughter.
They may not mean to, but they do.
They do things they shouldn't ought'a
And shift the blame to rest on you.

But they're being mucked up by their kids
Brats in designer jeans and coats,
Whose lifestyle costs X thousand quids
Ungracious louts on whom mother dotes.

Parents raise their own destruction.
They smile at you and make their plans.
'Just sign this dad, don't make ructions',
And so your home ends in their hands.

with apologies to Philip Larkin

On 'being a burden'

A lot of people as they get older worry that they 'don't want to be a burden on their children in their old age'. This is a short-sighted and foolish attitude. It is far more useful, productive and appropriate to worry about not being enough of a burden on your children.

After all, weren't they a burden on you for long enough?

A few examples follow.

The burden of infirmity

Without doubt this is the big one. It's the fear that as we age, something in our body, or our mind, will call 'Time, gentlemen please' ahead of schedule. Naturally you end up worrying, 'Oh my God, who will look after me?'

But what you must never forget is that the fear is just as real for your children. Although they probably phrase it slightly differently. As in 'Oh my God, I've got to look after them!'

So, in the words of another one of those irritating self-help manuals, *Feel the Fear and Do It Anyway*. In other words, pretend to be infirm and watch the fun develop.

As an added bonus, seeing how your children react is a great way of deciding who gets what in the will.

A financial burden

This is the second pillar of burdenry. What you need to do is let your offspring know that as your latter years approach you are somewhat devoid of savings. And pension plans. And financial sense.

Alternatively you can finesse the stress you engender by reassuring your children that you have provided for your old age by investing all your savings in undeniably sound ventures that promise excellent returns. For example ostrich farms, internet start-ups or a vast array of 'collector's item, limited edition' plates issued by The Franklin Mint featuring 'Kittens In A Kerfuffle'.

That should put their minds at ease.

It's not just the secret of good comedy

The third key aspect of Being A Burden is timing. You must aim to reveal your problems at the time that will most inconvenience the plans and lives of your children. For example, a sudden attack of infirmity just before they're about to go away on holiday is always a winner. But the Holy Grail of the whole affair is to conjure up the prospect of a long-term, serious and worsening condition at that moment when your children are thinking of moving house.

Should your resolve ever weaken in any matters relating to Being A Burden, draw succour and resolve from the master of the art. Buy yourself a video of *Steptoe and Son*. Ideally track down the one where Harold is about to get married to 'a right gorgeous dolly bird'. Then watch how Old Man Steptoe outmanoeuvres his son. Genius. Pure genius.

A word of warning

From this point on, death, The Big D, features heavily. If you are easily offended it's probably best that you stop reading now. Mind you, if you are easily offended you probably stopped reading a long time ago.

Last words: a few first thoughts

Don't leave these to chance. Have something sorted out well in advance. Or you'll end up like Luther Burbank the famous American horticulturist.* His last words were 'I don't feel good.' Accurate, but hardly profound.

The big problem is how do you know they're going to be your last words? What if you deliver your last line, then don't die? Do you hang around in silence? Or do you ask for that cup of tea or pillow, and run the risk of these becoming your last words?

Your best bet is to choose something and have it written down somewhere. Or printed on a T-shirt. Or better still, tattooed on the inside of your left thigh.

* Oh come on, everyone knows at least three famous American horticulturists.

Last words: a few second thoughts

OK, so coming up with your own last words is no easy task. So to help inspire you I'll just mention the famous last words I've found most apposite, profound and moving. They come from Conrad Hilton, the man who started with next to nothing and built the chain of hotels that bears his name. Just before he died he was asked if he had any last words of wisdom for the world. And he did.

'Leave the shower curtain on the inside of the tub.'

Now who could argue with that?

Preparing for the big day

Why should the people you leave behind have all the fun? They get to decide the date. They get to send out the invitations. They get to choose the music. They get to pick the food.

They even get to decide on what handles to put on the coffin.

I mention the handles on the coffin thing because it was a choice I was confronted with when my father died. So there I was sitting in a gloomy office, still pretty much numb with shock, having to decide whether to go for the simple or the more rococo option handlewise. In the end we went for the simple brass handles. And I found myself thinking the thought all of us comfort ourselves with in such circumstances 'It's what he would have wanted.'

Only much later did I really think that line

of reasoning through and come to the conclusion that I had no idea what 'he would have wanted' for his own funeral. Maybe he didn't want something simple. Maybe he wanted to parade down the street behind a New Orleans marching band. Maybe he wanted that whole Dickensian deal with a top-hatted geezer leading two black plumed horses. Or maybe he wanted to be buried in a field beneath an olive tree.

So to spare your nearest and dearest such dilemmas at what will necessarily be a somewhat fraught time in their lives, why not have the whole shebang sorted out well in advance? That way 'what he/she would have wanted' will be abundantly clear because it will be down in black and white.

Now once you get your head around the concept of arranging your own funeral it is but a short step to realising that, seeing as it is your last big party, why not have a little fun with it?

The Baroque Funeral

The Baroque Funeral is the full on, OTT, Liberace-style affair. For this you need a hand-carved, completely gilded, mahogany coffin carried in by six large body-builders clad in flouncy Louis XV frippery, all crying. Atop the coffin should be a floral arrangement that stands taller than you (when you were still around to stand) and that should be based on some pretentious theme like 'Truth and Beauty' or 'The Good Samaritan' or 'Blair and Mandelson: The Love of Tyranny or the Tyranny of Love?'

As the coffin is brought into the church – sorry, cathedral – a fanfare of trumpets should play your favourite Kylie song (I recommend 'I Should Be So Lucky') and a bejewelled midget should back away from it strewing rose petals in its path. The eulogy should be lifted

180

from Shakespeare and be read by the likes of Sir Ian McKellen or Dale Winton. And little girls dressed as Victorian shepherdesses should wander among the pews offering mourners silken handkerchiefs embroidered with a list of your achievements.

After the cremation, four Nubian warriors clad only in loincloths should arrive upon thoroughbred Arabian stallions to carry your ashes to the four corners of the globe. And as for the catering back at the marquee, start with individual spam soufflés; include at least one dish whose ingredients have to be flown in from abroad that very morning; and for pudding hire Delia, Nigella and Jamie to don Crimplene and Velcro basques and weep while handing out napkins and reclining amidst a full-scale recreation of the Trevi Fountain made out of both white and dark chocolate.

That should make the point.

The Minimalist Funeral

The Minimalist Funeral is somewhat of a contrast to the Baroque Funeral.

No coffin, just a body bag. No official cars, just complimentary one-day bus passes. No special music, just low, atonal humming. And no flowers, just the subtle suggestiveness of an elegantly lit empty vase.

As for the service/eulogy something along these lines will more than suffice:

'John Smith, born, lived, died, missed.'

Back at the house toast and tap water should be more than enough to offer mourners.

The Slapstick Funeral

For this you need to choose and position your
pallbearers very carefully. On one side of your
coffin have very tall people, on the other side
very short people. Replace the kneeling
cushions in the church with whoopee cushions.

Request no flowers, but flour instead, and
instruct the mourners to throw handfuls of the
stuff at each other as the coffin passes. Employ a
blubbing clown to patrol the aisles with a water
pistol squirting water in the eyes of anyone not
crying enough. And have the theme tune to the
Benny Hill Show (the one where he chases
scantily clad young girls at double speed) played
as the coffin leaves the church.

At the reception lay on copious amounts of
champagne in bottles that have been well and
truly shaken up. And serve the drinks
accompanied by large custard pies.

The Soap Opera Funeral

To carry this out successfully you need to get in touch with a theatrical agency and hire an actor. If you're a man, choose the most stunning looking woman you can find and hire an all-black outfit that oozes sensuality with just a hint of wild sordidness. If you're a woman, you need to track down an actor who is honed, buffed and more gorgeous looking than any mortal has the right to be. Then hire him tight black leather trousers, a clinging white T-shirt and a large, throbbing, motorbike.

Of course, it's vital that you tell no-one that you're doing any of this. In fact, it's vital that the funeral carries on completely normally at all times. Until the right moment comes. Then as everyone is sitting down in the church or chapel or wherever, have your actor make their entrance. So the mysterious woman in black enters, walks up the aisle, places a single red rose and a pair of handcuffs on your coffin, then turns and walks away with a tear in her eye. The actor does the same, except he rides up on the motorbike.

Leave no explanation anywhere as to who these people are, or why they should be heartbroken at your demise.

The Surreal Funeral

Again no flowers. Instead ask for bouquets of fish. Instead of a eulogy arrange for a tax inspector to read out a randomly chosen page from the Argos catalogue. For the music get a string quartet of blind musicians to come in and tune their instruments. As for the coffin, have one made out of something soft and malleable like plasticine or something that will start to melt at room temperature like frozen Brie.

As a finishing touch, only invite people you never knew.

The 'Changing Tombs' Funeral

Finally, why not save your relatives the stress of sorting out the whole affair by getting your neighbours to arrange your funeral with just a little help from Carole Smillie and Lawrence Llewellyn Bowen?

(Just a wild guess here, but you might well end up with a lilac coffin made up of MDF.)

But enough about funerals – instead let's just nail that one great last lie, you know, the one that says 'You can't take it with you'

After your demise, arrange for all your assets to be turned into cash. Then arrange for the cash to line your coffin. Then specify cremation. But keep all this a secret from your family and friends until that moment when the coffin slides ever so serenely through those little curtains.

Well, they should all have been nicer to you when you were alive, shouldn't they?

Outroduction

I leave this to the words of John Webster, the fifteenth-century English poet:

> Is not old wine wholesomest, old pippins the
>   toothsomest?
> Does not old wood burn brightest, old linen
>   wash whitest?
> Old soldiers, sweetest, are surest, and old lovers
>   soundest.

But then again he died aged 42, so what did he know?